# What Is an Attribute?

Nancy Kelly Allen

ROURKE PUBLISHING

www.rourkepublishing.com

www.rourkepublishing.com

PHOTO CREDITS: Cover: © Buruhtan; Title Page: © Mark Evans; Page 3: © Anna Baburkina; Page 5: © Paul Rosado, © Jenna Wagner, © paul hill, © Clint Scholz; Page 7, 9: © Len Green, © Lbarn, © Derris Lanier; Page 11, 13: © picsfive; Page 15, 17: © Robert Wilson, © Richard Hoffkins; Page 19, 21: © Claudio Monni; Page 23: © Tor Lindqvist

Edited by Kelli L. Hicks

Cover and Interior design by Tara Raymo

## Library of Congress Cataloging-in-Publication Data

Allen, Nancy Kelly, 1949-
 What is an attribute? / Nancy Kelly Allen.
    p. cm. -- (Little world math concepts)
 Includes bibliographical references and index.
 ISBN 978-1-61590-296-5 (Hard Cover) (alk. paper)
 ISBN 978-1-61590-535-5 (Soft Cover)
 1. Mathematical notation--Juvenile literature. 2. Mathematical notation. I. Title.
 QA41.A45 2011
 511.3'2--dc22
                              2010009610

Rourke Publishing
Printed in the United States of America, North Mankato, Minnesota
033010
033010LP

www.rourkepublishing.com - rourke@rourkepublishing.com
Post Office Box 643328 Vero Beach, Florida 32964

Is it red? Is it blue? Is it big? Is it small? What is an attribute?

An attribute shows how things are alike and different.

# Alike          # Different

Which two cars are alike?

The cars with the attribute of yellow are alike.

**Alike**

Which two cars are different?

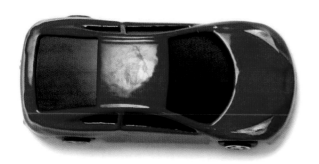

The cars with attributes of green and red are different.

# Different

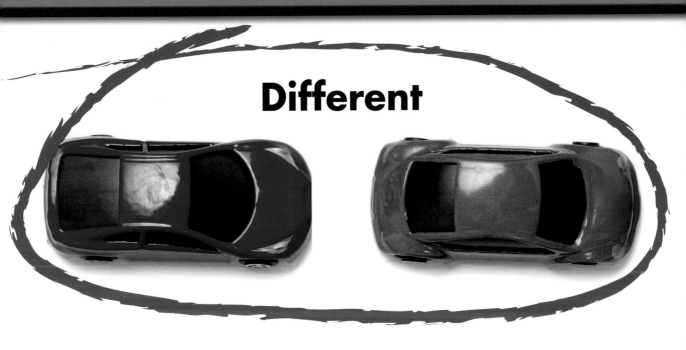

Which car is big? Honk! Honk!

The car with the attribute of big is circled.

**Big**

Which car is small? Beep! Beep!

The car with the attribute of small is circled.

**Small**

Can you find the cars with the same attributes?

# Index

## Websites

www.coolmath-games.com/0-bloons-pop-3/index.html

www.crayola.com/free-coloring-pages/cars-trucks-and-other-
   vehicles-coloring-pages/

www.thekidzpage.com/learninggames/shapes.html

## About the Author

Nancy Kelly Allen lives in a small house surrounded by big hills in Kentucky. In spring and summer, the hills are green. In autumn, the hills are red, yellow, and brown. In winter, the hills are white. Nancy lives with two little, black schnauzers that give big, pink kisses.